101 Leadership Actions

for

Creating and Managing Virtual Teams

Ollie Malone, Ph.D.

HRD Press • Amherst • Massachusetts

Published by:

HRD Press
22 Amherst Road
Amherst, MA 01002
1-800-822-2801 (U.S. and Canada)
413-253-3488
413-253-3490 (FAX)
www.hrdpress.com

ISBN 0-87425-810-3

Cover design by ZenGator Productions
Editorial services by Sally Farnham
Production services by PerfecType

Printed in Canada

Table of Contents

Preface	1
How This Book Is Organized	3
Using This Book Effectively	7
Strategy and Virtual Teams	9
Structure and Virtual Teams	30
The Practices of Virtual Teams	42
The Tools of Virtual Teams	88
Managing Virtual Teams	102
Technology and Virtual Teams	127
Systems and Virtual Teams	146
What's Next with Your Virtual Team?	159

Preface

Unlike any time in the past, virtual teams are now a way of life in most organizations in corporate America. A number of factors are influencing the proliferation of these virtual work teams, including:

- Mergers and acquisitions where employees are retained in multiple locations, rather than simply relocated to another central work location.
- An increase in the number of employees who telecommute and work flexible hours, which often means that team members do not see each other or interact regularly on a face-to-face basis.
- The use of temporary or ad hoc teams formed to address a specific work need or issue and then reformed into different teams for future work projects.

- The use of temporary employees or consultants who might not be co-located with the projects they are supporting.
- Medical or other health-related issues that prevent an employee from being physically present with his or her team, but with new technology, can still contribute to the team's goal.
- Employees with physical challenges such as hearing loss, vision loss, or difficulties with mobility who cannot fully participate on a team, but might be able to do more with the help of new technology.
- The use of "experts" whose short-term involvement on a team does not require them to be physically present for all of the team's work.

All these factors make virtual teams a more common reality than at any time in the past.

How This Book
Is Organized

This book is designed to be a resource that will assist you in managing, leading, or participating in a virtual team. Whatever your role within the virtual team, this book will provide you with new ideas, practices, and suggestions to help your virtual team be more effective.

This book is divided into seven sections, each of which addresses planning considerations for virtual-team performance. These areas include:

- *Strategy.* Strategy has to focus on the "big picture," which is of particular importance to leaders who are forming or justifying virtual teams. In this section, you will find a number of ideas that should be helpful as you build your case for virtual teams and lay the cornerstones of the foundation for virtual teams.

- **Structure.** What is the most appropriate structure for virtual teams? What factors should be considered in making such a decision? These are the types of issues that will be examined in the structure section.
- **Practices.** In this section, you will find a number of ideas based on the work of numerous successful virtual teams that can motivate virtual team members to consider and implement practices that will make their team successful.
- **Tools.** Tools are just what they suggest—"quick hitters" that enable you to make things happen with your virtual teams. In this section, we outline how the best tools available can help you and your teams.
- **Management.** What should the supervisor, manager, or leader do? Virtual teams might not have been covered in the management training you received. In this section, we will address some of the unique challenges for managers of virtual teams. We will also address some of the things that you, the leader, might need to do differently with your virtual team employees than you do with your on-site team employees.
- **Technology.** Technology provides a means of connecting virtual team members. This sec-

tion will outline several technology principles useful for virtual teams. This section does not review all the potential technology available to virtual teams; there are far too many possibilities, and the list changes just about every day. You will, however, find some general guidelines in this section that should help you make good decisions relative to the use of technology.

- *Systems.* Finally, we will address some of the systems that need to be in place in order to support effective virtual teams.

Using this Book
Effectively

Think of this book not as a "How to" book, but a "What to do" book. It acts as a ready reference for leaders and team members in building strong virtual teams. As such, it should:

- Provide ideas for getting started with virtual teams by identifying some of the key considerations necessary for the teams' initial successes.
- Provide ideas for team members who have not yet decided to be a part of a virtual team. What are some of the issues that virtual team members face? Does this potential team member have the knowledge, skills, and attitude to work effectively in a virtual team environment?
- Provide ideas for those who support virtual

teams. If they are aware of the key challenges faced by the virtual team, support people can more effectively create work around solutions or identify means of adapting present solutions for the benefit of virtual teams.

- Provide ideas for managers of virtual teams. Virtual team managers are quite different from other management groups. If a team is to be successful, it will be so largely because of the manager's initiative in paying attention to the virtual team, to identifying and addressing issues that block the virtual team's success, and in managing the performance of the virtual team in such a way that the issues of space and distance do not hinder top-flight performance and the recognition thereof.

Strategy and Virtual Teams

Building effective virtual teams means fundamentally making sure that the teams you create are considered an important part of the organization by everyone within the organization, at all levels.

As such, your virtual teams should be considered as critical to the organization's success as any other teams in current operation. The following information should be clearly communicated to the whole organization:

- The virtual teams' purposes for being
- How the virtual teams' work fits in with the overall mission and vision of the organization
- How the virtual teams will be evaluated

As you create clarity at all levels of your organization, you will build a platform for success with regard to your virtual teams. Rather than being seen as "necessary evils" in the organization, virtual teams will be considered critical team players in and among the many initiatives that will be used to create success.

1

Develop a clear business strategy.

If your organization doesn't have a clear business strategy, your virtual teams are doomed to failure before they begin. A clear business strategy is not just for the benefit of your virtual teams, however; a clear business strategy benefits the entire organization by communicating where you are headed and giving teams a general sense of how much of a gap exists between where you are and where you need to be. A clear business strategy provides some level of direction in terms of how your team should go about closing the performance gap.

All of this information will help your teams focus their energies in order to achieve the outcomes most desired. This clear business strategy will help release your employees' creativity so that they can engage their thoughts and suggestions in the organization's overall efforts.

2

Provide "line of sight."

"Line of sight" is a term that relates to the employee's ability to see a clear connection between his or her work and the organization's overall strategy and direction.

Line of sight assists employees in having clear justification and purpose for the work they are doing. It should also enable your employees to identify ways of not only performing the work at hand, but improving their individual tasks so that the overall goal is also improved. Finally, line of sight enables your employees to see themselves as a larger part of the company's operation.

When you create line of sight, you should map out your processes or draw a work process flow chart from the point of the employee's involvement until the work reaches the customer or up to the point where what the employee does impacts the organization's overall strategy.

3

Make the whole visible to everyone.

A number of tools are being used today to help all employees gain a more strategic view of their work within the context of the organization's overall work. If you have access to these types of resources, take full advantage of them.

Some of these resources that help people take a strategic view of the whole include:

- Videotapes or presentations that show how the work flows from one area to another until it is complete.
- Process maps that use block diagrams and

demonstrate the flow of work from one part of the organization to the other.

- Visual maps that are drawn by individuals with artistic skills. These visual maps include icons or other representations of the various players in the overall process, which help everyone remember who is involved in the work and at what stage.
- Organizational "field trips," where individuals can see how the work flows by walking through the various phases of the work process.
- Self-guided tours through the organization. Such tours accomplish what organizational "field trips" do, but they are done individually rather than with a small group.

4

Stimulate rich conversations within your organization.

So-called rich conversations elicit thinking that goes beyond the day-to-day, what-do-we-absolutely-need-to-do considerations, looking deeper into the organization. These rich conversations ask questions such as, "Why do we need to do this?" "What would happen if we didn't do this?" "What would happen if we did this differently than we may have done in the past?"

The purpose of these rich conversations is to

open up the thinking of your team members in such a way that they challenge every aspect of your operation and are able to find new and improved ways of working and achieving your team's goals.

5

Develop a clear purpose and focus for the team.

How does this team's purpose and focus fit into the larger strategy of the organization? How well can members of the team articulate that vision and focus? Are they able to make sense of their purpose in light of other broader organizational considerations?

Do team members appear to have taken ownership of the vision and purpose of the group? Or are they simply doing what they are told?

Ultimately, the goal of the team leader and every team member is to ensure that every person who works to accomplish the team's goals does so with a strong sense of ownership.

6

Develop clear objectives for the team.

Your employees' ability to own and embrace the vision for the company and the team will to a significant extent be based on their ability to embrace their own vision of what they will contribute. You must develop team goals, but your employees will have to identify creative ways of achieving their own goals and tracking their overall performance toward the goals.

The sooner you are able to help your team develop its goals, the sooner you will be able to start realizing some of the benefits that result from the team's full investment in the achievement of the organization's goals.

7

Develop clear objectives for individuals on the team.

Some of your goals will be accomplished as a result of a team working together to accomplish them, but a good number of your goals will be achieved as a result of employees doing their individual tasks at a consistently high level of performance throughout the year.

Once individual goals are developed, encourage group brainstorming and idea sharing with regard to the ways in which clear objectives can be reviewed. This is particularly valuable with regard to team members who are not located in the same vicinity. By sharing ideas, team members are learning to work effectively together, solve problems, and give and receive effective feedback.

8

Encourage carefully chosen small steps initially.

It is difficult to consistently make huge achievements throughout the course of a team's "journey" to its end goal. In truth, huge achievements are typically the result of a number of small things being done exceptionally well.

Taking small incremental steps will enable you to learn as you go and to share the wealth of knowledge that is being developed with other members of the team who could benefit by the new insights.

Light a "fire in the belly."

Identifying the work "passions" that drive the members of your team and encouraging them to move into these areas is an art that effective leaders develop over time. By observing your employees— what they like to do, what they don't like to do, where they seem to shine, and where they have the greatest organizational impact—you will be much better able to identify each employee's "fire."

Encourage these employees to take initiative in the areas where their "fire" exists, and you will enable individuals to move in areas of strength— areas where the individual is able to work at a far faster pace than is otherwise possible. Passion makes the difference!

10

Identify the benefits of virtual teams.

As each virtual team begins to work together, encourage members to consider what they believe to be some of the benefits of *not* being co-located. Then ask your teams how they can take advantage of these benefits to create an even greater organizational outcome.

11

Identify the liabilities of virtual teams.

What are the potholes and pitfalls that your virtual team might face?

Are team members in different time zones? If so, time will be an issue. What is the potential impact of not having everyone in the same time zone?

Are there physical limitations at any of the sites that need to be overcome?

Having generated these considerations, identify commitments that need to be made in order to overcome these potential potholes and pitfalls.

12

Solicit the support of top management.

Occasionally, one virtual team will require a bit more help than the others. Top management's involvement might prove useful.

In general, teams should do their initial groundwork before seeking the help of top management. The team should consider the organization's overall strategy and the strategy and goals of their team, as well as what the benefits and potential pitfalls and potholes are to working together virtually.

When these have been identified, specific requests can be made of top management for support in specific areas. Some of the areas in which top management support is often sought include:

- Funding
- Open and supportive communication about the team and its importance to the organization
- Removal of organizational roadblocks that hinder high performance
- Intervention with other groups whose buy-in and/or support might be essential to long-term success
- Visible interaction with the team in order to demonstrate personal interest and encouragement

Structure and Virtual Teams

Within a virtual team, structure serves two important functions:

- First, it influences work flow—how work progresses from one part of the team to another so that it can be completed effectively and as efficiently as possible.
- Second, it focuses on the relationships between smaller sub-units of your teams—the two- and three-person relationships that are essential for your success.

As you think about structure, then, give attention to the macro issues—the department-to-department and big-picture items. Be sure to pay attention to some of the smaller "micro" issues that relate to the inner workings of your team and the work flow among team members.

When you have both the macro and micro team issues addressed, you will have a team that is moving toward significant high performance.

13

Eliminate the hierarchy.

Over the past 20 years, hierarchy has come under an increased level of scrutiny. Is it really needed? What does it add to the work you are charged with doing? If one or more layers in the hierarchy of the organization were eliminated, how would this affect the work product with which you are charged?

These are the types of questions that are worth investing time and energy to answer. When you have the answers, you will be closer to determining the true value of the hierarchy you have in place. And you will be closer to determining how much of your resources currently devoted to the maintenance of the present hierarchy would more effectively be used to produce better quality results.

Establish position or group status of members and define task roles of group members.

This might sound like a recommendation to create fiefdoms, but in truth, it is a recommendation for the creation of clear roles and responsibilities for those who work on your virtual team. These clear roles and responsibilities will save time and energy and will promote the development of resources within the virtual team that can address issues important to the team's overall performance.

As much as possible, make sure that team members have some sort of designated role. This will create a sense of ownership on the part of all your team members, and it will allow each member to develop a particular expertise that should be useful to the team as a whole.

15

Establish some work rules.

What is the best way to do the work you are charged with doing? What are the specific steps, actions, or tasks an individual should do to function well in your department or in a given role?

Because your team is not in the same room (and possibly not even on the same continent), it will be important to establish, early on, rules for the way work is to be done so that regardless of a team member's location, there can be a level of assurance that everyone is operating from the same set of expectations and procedures.

Once these work rules are identified, write them

down and make sure everyone in the department (and anyone else who could derive benefit) clearly understands the procedures, steps, and processes.

16

Consider the issue of location.

You might have a few team members who work at the same site. How is their work space configured? Is it structured in such a way that communication and information exchange is optimum? If not, consider making a change to facilitate open dialogue.

The question of hard walls versus cubicles versus open offices also emerges. Make a conscious and intentional decision about the team's physical configuration after you consider your strategy, the work processes that you support, your annual goals, and the input from other members of the team.

As you examine these factors, the best arrangement to facilitate optimal outcomes should become clearer.

Your decision should not be based on anyone's desire for "privacy." A high degree of individual privacy is highly correlated with a decrease in work-related focus and productivity—something to keep in mind when you consider where the members of virtual teams will work.

17

Create a formal meeting structure.

Virtual teams, unlike face-to-face teams, typically need a much more formal structure. This more formal structure is designed to ensure that all important issues are dealt with, that time is used well, and that there is a balance of input among all team members.

A significant level of responsibility for this structure falls on the team's leader, who needs to be skillful in managing not only the content of the meeting, but the meeting's processes and outcomes as well.

18

Regularly redesign your meeting structure.

The risk of having a formal meeting structure is that it can become too familiar, too hum-drum, and too easy for participants to fade in and out of.

In order to minimize the likelihood of this occurring, redesign your meeting structure every 5 to 10 meetings. The redesign can be as simple as beginning with those things that used to constitute the ending parts of the agenda, but the redesign can also be a wholesale restructuring of the elements of the meeting and its content.

Whatever the decision, make sure every team member is aware of the new structure and is prepared to participate in the dialogue.

The Practices of
Virtual Teams

Whatever an individual's role is in a virtual team—team member, team leader, team sponsor, senior executive, facilitator, or consultant—engaging in certain proven practices will help the team reach its potential.

The next several pages focus on the practices of highly effective virtual teams that enable them to achieve their goals, while they build effective interaction among their individual members.

19

Explain rules, define terminology, and use explicit language and descriptions.

All communities, large and small, create unique ways of interacting with one another that are not known to those who are not a part of the community. For example, a common word such as *soda* has very different meanings in different parts of the United States.

The complexity of language and regional variations make it difficult for people from different parts of the country (not to mention the world) to communicate effectively.

In an effort to break down the barriers that exist between virtual team members, develop the habit of using clear, explicit language, and avoid the use of acronyms unless you are willing to define these acronyms the first few times they are used.

Rules and practices, likewise, are often unique to one group or one location. Spell out these rules and practices for the benefit of those who might not be familiar with them.

20

Foster social presence.

Invisibility on a virtual team can occur easily, but it can be quite costly when it affects the quality and quantity of the team's results. Make sure that your team members know each other, even if you have to re-introduce team members to one another, and continue to create additional connections between individual members of the team.

Use formal and informal interactions among your team members to strengthen the members' familiarity with one another (including job strengths) and the team's ability to work together.

21

Establish norms for group interaction.

Norms describe how people want to work together. They consist of value descriptions such as "open," "honest," and "direct" that are important to the team.

As soon as possible, take the time to identify these norms. As a general rule, there should be between five and seven norms.

22

Evaluate your team's performance against the norms members have chosen.

Norms are worthless if your team isn't actively working to live up to them. Make sure that the norms chosen have "teeth" and are being adhered to by your team.

Where necessary, either reinforce, remove, or reconsider your team's norms to make sure that they are up-to-date and relevant and that they have the team's full commitment.

23

Establish a creating stage for your team's work.

The creating stage is the foundation for team members' involvement and contribution. The creating stage should include:

- An *orientation* to the nature and purpose of the team (Why is the team here?)
- An *introduction* to the team's members (Who am I? Who are you?)
- Team *interaction* (initial building of trust)
- Goal/role *classification* (What's my role? What is the role of others here?)

24

Establish procedures for group discussion.

A decision-making procedure should be established for virtual groups. Effective groups go through stages such as *conception* (clarifying the idea or issue), *generation* (identifying causes of and solutions to the issue), *reduction* (narrowing down the possibilities), *selection* (picking the most likely solution), *implementation* (acting on the chosen solution), and *evaluation* (determining if the chosen solution has addressed the issue).

25

Establish rules of "netiquette" and create an active list of "ebbreviations."

All teams need rules and norms, but virtual teams need "netiquette"—a set of guidelines for the team's online interactions. These rules will be useful to new team members, as well as to other individuals who are actively involved in the team's work.

26

Create a newspaper-style report after each meeting, and publish it for the rest of the team.

Follow the style used by journalists to report on a meeting: Focus on the Who, What, When, Where, Why, and How.

Using this style will enable you to cover the most important facts clearly and succinctly.

27

Encourage the team to acknowledge who is present and who is absent at the beginning of every meeting,

and develop clear strategies for involving all members in the team's work.

Involving each member in the team's work and maintaining regular communication with all members (regardless of meeting attendance) keep everyone connected.

Formally noting who is not present will help the leader remember to communicate with these members so that everything stays on track.

28

Develop a team policy of sending out "hot news" bulletins.

"Hot news" bulletins are a good way for the team to stay in touch with one another, know what is going on, and celebrate accomplishments toward the team's goals.

29

Create ways to celebrate accomplishments as a team, even when the team is not physically together.

Making sure the entire team participates in team celebrations reinforces the "team-ness" of their work. Some organizations celebrate via teleconference, but standard conference calls are also useful. Symbolic toasts are another means by which teams can celebrate major milestones.

30

Use "information mapping" to communicate information.

Information mapping is a way of structuring information so that it can be read and understood quickly and easily.

Create your own format so that team members are able to read through every piece of communication quickly and understand how to appropriately respond or take any action that is important.

31

Amplify energy.

All teams lose focus and energy over time. Amplifying energy is a way to reenergize the team so that it is able to continue on a productive course.

Any team member can reenergize the team—it is not the exclusive responsibility of the team leader, supervisor, or manager. Some individuals have the ability to reenergize groups of people through the use of jokes, team exercises, or even something so basic as lively conversation. Team members who possess these talents should be encouraged to put them to good use on behalf of the team.

32

Establish regular communication practices as a means of avoiding communication gaps.

Regular communication allows teams to create the rhythms that are essential to high performance.

Establish a regular meeting day and time, and

keep meetings the same length as a way of disciplining the team to focus on the importance of regular communication. Once you establish a schedule, stick to it and encourage all members of the team to contribute to the content and quality of the communication.

33

Establish agreeable guidelines regarding team communication.

Once an e-mail, fax, telephone call, or other form of communication is received from a team member, how long should an individual wait for a response before following up? For some, "within 24 hours" is reasonable, while for others, "24 to 72 hours" is reasonable.

Agree on what constitutes "reasonable" within your group. Make sure your team understands it and sticks to it.

34

Monitor and manage communication effectiveness.

How well is your group communicating? Is the communication clear, timely, and focused? Does it accomplish what is needed?

Periodically (more often in the beginning), monitor the effectiveness of your group's communication so that everyone develops good habits of communication within the team.

35

Stimulate communication within the network of team members.

Inevitably, team members who are in contact with networks of other people receive information that is useful to other members of their team. When this occurs, information should be passed on to those who can benefit from the information.

This is not solely the responsibility of management. Each person on the team should share relevant information in a timely manner if it is not of a confidential nature and reciprocate to maintain a flow of accurate and useful communication.

Build trust in your virtual team based on proven performance, rather than on social bonds.

One definition of *trust* is "a belief in the competence of another." As you build your virtual team, extend trust to those who have demonstrated that

they are trustworthy—the individuals who perform their work on time and within the standards
of quality established by your team.

These are the individuals who are worthy of
your trust.

37

Create a virtual environment of inclusiveness and involvement.

In an environment where everyone is physically present, being "out of the loop" is something that most people can easily overcome. Individuals can get caught up "through the grapevine," around the water cooler, or in other less-direct ways. In a virtual environment, not having all the information is a bit more difficult to remedy, since there is no "water cooler" or other social means of informally sharing information.

Make sure all your virtual team members have all the information they need.

38

Creative approaches for providing feedback, coaching, and support for the virtual team.

Many of the typical approaches for providing feedback, coaching, and active support to team members will not work in a virtual environment.

Identify new approaches that take advantage of the virtual environment. For example, consider sending electronic cards to your team members through one of the free online services that provide such cards.

There are dozens of other ways to show appreciation and recognize employees within a virtual setting.

39

Encourage team members to develop interpersonal relationships.

It is particularly difficult in virtual teams to develop interpersonal relationships—relationships where people are able to get to know each other and, on the basis of that knowledge, develop a greater level of comfort and confidence in each other.

It might be necessary for you to structure a

"virtual happy hour" where individuals can have unstructured time to get to know each other socially the way they would if they were co-located. Be sure to manage these "happy hours" responsibly with regard to company policies and standard-and-accepted business practices.

40

Clarify goals at every meeting.

It should be expected that whenever your virtual team gets together, it does so to accomplish something. Explicitly state the goal (or goals) of the meetings you have. Do this at the beginning of the meeting and, if necessary, return to that goal at various points in the meeting to ensure that the meeting is progressing toward the achievement of the goal.

Finally, at the end of the meeting, determine the degree to which you and your team believe you have achieved the goal you set out to achieve.

41

Develop visual, online reminders of the progress being made toward important goals, tasks, and projects.

The availability of software for the creation of charts and graphs makes it possible for every team to develop and publish graphic representations of their work and progress to date.

Ensure that these charts and graphs are updated and that the date is visibly displayed on the chart so that team members know the current status of tasks and projects.

42

Keep team interactions upbeat and action oriented.

A common complaint about many teams is that when they get together, all they do is complain about *what is,* rather than creatively consider *what could be.* Do not allow your team to fall into this trap.

If your team is tempted to "sing the blues," interrupt the negative dialogue with a question, such as "So, what are we going to do about this?" or "How can we address this problem and move on?"

As team members develop the discipline of action orientation, their problem-solving skills will improve and the quality of the results will skyrocket.

43

Standardize common protocols.

"How do you do 'X'?" is a common question many workers ask. In other words, "What's the standard protocol for addressing this situation?" If your team has taken the time to write down its standard protocols, the task of orientation and initial skill building is made that much easier.

Make sure the common activities done on your team are written down clearly so that everyone—both those who are new to the team and those who are well-established on the team—are able to follow the procedures effectively.

44

Celebrate the achievement of milestones.

One strategy seldom used by teams is to celebrate milestones. These milestones could be significant steps toward the achievement of a major goal, or they could include a notable achievement essential for longer-term success.

Whatever the milestone, take a moment to celebrate it. This will give your team the opportunity to get energized as they reflect on the most recent success and consider the challenges that lie ahead.

45

Identify the barriers to collaboration that your team needs to overcome.

Most teams encounter difficulties as they attempt to achieve success. The most successful teams are able to identify these difficulties, create a plan to address them, implement the plan, and move forward successfully.

What is standing in the way of your team's success?

46

Identify what people should do in the event of a crisis.

No one wishes for a crisis, but smart teams know that by preparing for one, they will be in a better position to address one should it occur.

Develop a crisis recovery plan for your team and ensure that every person on your team knows the plan and is able to implement it. You may never need it, but in the event that you do, you will be glad you have it.

47

Assume nothing, but spell out everything.

This blanket statement is based on the fact that it is difficult to get two people to assume the same things. Add the issue of space, geography, and different tasks to the mix, and assumptions become potentially lethal.

There are many areas of work performance that need to be stated explicitly for the benefit of all. There might also be other areas relative to team interaction, team problem solving, or team communication that are important to write down.

48

Watch for conflict.

Conflict is sometimes easy to spot, while at other times it goes unnoticed. Develop keen radar for the presence of conflict in your virtual team. It might emerge around ideas (which idea is right, best, most appropriate, etc.), or it might develop around personalities (who likes whom, who doesn't like whom). Whatever the source, conflict is a major barrier to team effectiveness.

49

Effectively manage conflict.

If there are signs of significant conflict (i.e., conflict that is hindering the team's achievement of its goals), it needs to be dealt with directly and forthrightly.

Occasionally, it might be useful to bring in a third party to assist in conflict management. The presence of another individual who is not in the middle of the conflict is often useful in gaining perspective about the conflict and what should be done with it.

50

Do better
next time.

Whatever your team is working on—a project, a party, a team-building activity—commit yourselves to doing that activity even better the next time it is undertaken.

This philosophy of continuous improvement will ensure that your team becomes stronger and better with every interaction.

51

Monitor and manage meeting behavior.

When your virtual team meets, who talks to whom? About what? Who is not included in team interactions? Who sits on the sidelines and doesn't appear interested in the work of the team?

Follow these behaviors and encourage those who might be on the fringes to get more involved. Encourage those who are involved to the point of excluding others to allow room for others to speak and offer their perspectives.

52

Consider obtaining the services of a meeting facilitator.

Getting a team to work together well is hard work. This hard work can be made easier by the presence of a third party known as a facilitator.

The facilitator ensures that the team moves toward the established goals, while at the same time maintains a high level of involvement on the part of all the team members.

The Tools of
Virtual Teams

This section identifies a number of tools that can help your team work efficiently and effectively.

The tools that are listed here do not constitute an exhaustive list. They are included to stimulate the consideration of other possibilities that could help your team excel.

53

Create a sign, a logo, or a symbol to represent your team.

Even if your team consists of only one member, the presence of a visual identifier reinforces the identity of the team.

If team members are physically located near people who are not part of their own team, the visual identifier can create a boundary between their team and members of other teams, as well as remind them of their team connection.

54

Make your team members aware of the rules for online communication.

Online communication is unique in that we cannot make use of nonverbal cues, voice inflection, or other ways to decipher the meaning of another person's communication.

That being the case, online communication must be far more precise than other forms of communication.

Provide your team members with guidelines or a checklist that will be helpful when communicating online.

Provide extensive training in virtual teamwork to help overcome process loss.

There are few experts in the area of virtual teamwork. For that reason, most of your team members will be learning as they go. Make sure your team members have both the orientation to virtual teams (what they are and how they differ from other teams) and the skills of virtual teamwork.

Conducting this training prior to implementing virtual teams will likely reduce levels of frustration, ineffectiveness, and poor initial productivity.

56

Develop tools for the selection of high-quality virtual team members.

Because the virtual team is different, the selection process for virtual team members should be different from in-person selection processes.

Create real-life situations that reflect the work of your virtual team and ask candidates to participate in those situations. As they observe the candidates, the interviewers will have an idea of who is likely to adapt well to the virtual environment and who is likely to struggle. Candidates, as well, will have a clearer sense of their abilities and comfort level for working in this type of environment.

57

Create a shared virtual space where team members can interact beyond the scope of work.

Informal exchanges are useful in building trust and better relationships among team members. Ensure that these types of informal exchanges take place in your group and that individuals participate in them periodically.

58

Regularly consider the need for training.

The development of team skills will require team members to use learning skills that they might be unfamiliar with or rusty at.

Regular skill training will keep employees on their toes with regard to the latest technology, approaches, and methodology for getting their work done.

Review and align processes periodically.

Explicitly identifying processes, writing them down, measuring them, and evaluating them should be a priority for virtual teams.

As these processes are identified and refined, they provide a foundation for common approaches and high-quality outcomes.

60

Develop and make available a variety of job aids.

Job aids are simple tools that are posted at an employee's workspace for the purpose of reminding him or her how work is to be done, or how a particular task should be accomplished.

Given the complexity of many jobs, these job aids can be of great value to virtual team members.

If you use these job aids, ensure that they are accurate, updated often, and available to all team members.

61

Perform a readiness assessment.

Identify the factors that are most important to your virtual environment. Set the level of performance that is essential for your virtual teams. Finally, determine the "acceptable" point of performance to establish whether a virtual team should be formed.

After these tasks are completed, evaluate your current teams to determine how ready they are to become virtual teams.

Managing Virtual Teams

At the heart of every virtual team's effectiveness is management. Individuals working on virtual teams are, for the most part, experiencing a new way of working that is unfamiliar.

In addition, the management of these teams requires a different set of skills than those needed for management and supervisory roles. How do you "manage by walking around" on a virtual team? How do you get the right people "on the bus" and the wrong people "off the bus" in a virtual environment?

The art and the science of managing virtual teams will be the focus of the next collection of ideas. Examine them, use them, refine them, and expand them as you enter the world of virtual management.

62

Define team objectives.

What does this team exist to do? How can this team not only achieve its goals and objectives, but excel in that achievement? And how can the team not only excel at goal achievement, but do so in a virtual environment where the team's members don't feel as if they are estranged from one another?

As you think of your team's objectives, don't limit your consideration to the work itself. Obviously, the work is critical, but remember to consider other attributes that will help define virtual team excellence (i.e., the team's ability to work together and to identify and use unique virtual attributes for team success).

63

Identify appropriate team members.

The ability to function independently and effectively has to be close to the top of the list of criteria for members of a virtual team. Unlike co-located teams, the virtual team is fueled by a compelling set of goals and objectives and an energetic and committed team of individuals who can accomplish those goals and objectives.

Since working in a virtual environment is a relatively new phenomenon, it might be difficult to identify those who have previous experience. If so, look for individuals who are able to function well without immediate supervision, who are highly effective problem solvers, and who are able to network effectively with others to achieve a given outcome.

These three criteria should be useful in identifying virtual team members who will be able to move your agenda forward.

64

Establish a team leader.

Depending on the structure of your virtual team, having on-site team leaders can be a useful strategy. These individuals would possess go-to responsibilities so that questions relating to administrative matters or work process could be answered consistently.

If your compensation structure allows, provide financial incentive for individuals who perform these roles well.

65

Clarify the position of group members.

Who does what on your team? Who is the "go-to" person for one task or another? Who possesses expertise on a given work process or procedure? Clarifying the answers to these questions will help you expand accountability for your team's success to a number of individuals within the team.

Develop cross-team groups that are focused on particular skills.

Developing cross-team groups will keep team members from being isolated and help to develop broad competence across the team.

In addition, this will allow you to build in-house expertise on virtually every important business function.

67

Create in-house mentoring and coaching initiatives.

By creating cross-geography or cross-functional mentoring, you are strengthening the networks of interplay between team members.

Through these informal contacts and networks, individuals will not only know other team members better, but they will also have a greater sense of team members' expertise—and should be able to call on that expertise when needed.

68

Create ad hoc teams for unique tasks or opportunities.

Ad hoc teams afford team members the opportunity of working with individuals they might not have worked with before. These teams also provide opportunities to develop new skills and perspectives through the chemistry that is created by virtual team members.

69

Make sure that you understand and uphold the group's norms.

If the team's norms are not being adhered to, they are worthless. Yet team members, particularly in the team's early stages of operation, might be reluctant to speak out when clear violations of the norms are occurring.

By upholding these norms, management sets an example that team members should also be encouraged to emulate.

70

Take on the role of "chief communicator."

Ultimately, communication is everyone's responsibility, but team members might be unwilling to step up to the plate on this one until they see that communication is valued by the team.

Demonstrate that value. Create regular communication (at least weekly) and ensure that the content of the communication is worth listening to.

71

Find ways to spotlight individuals or small groups who are making exciting things happen.

Chances are there are a number of areas of team performance that are worth spotlighting. Goals are being achieved; individuals are accomplishing results in record-breaking time; quality is high; customers are expressing satisfaction about the work that is being done.

All of these things have a way of generating energy within the team—as long as they are well-publicized. Make sure they are.

72

If team members have not worked together in the past, allow time for them to get to know one another.

One option is to encourage team members to take "virtual lunches," where individuals in various locations spend their lunch times together online, exchanging information, asking questions, or engaging in small talk much like they would do in a face-to-face environment.

Team meetings, likewise, can include time for personal exchange so that virtual communication does not become overly sterile.

73

Make sure that your team members have a healthy balance of technical and interpersonal skills.

If you have inherited an existing team that will now be a virtual one, this might be a bit of a challenge since the team has already been established.

Nevertheless, helping your team members recognize the need for both technical and interpersonal skills and providing opportunities to develop these kinds of skill sets should be an item on your agenda.

74

Emphasize the need for commitment to the virtual team.

Face-to-face teams need commitment, and so do virtual teams. To solidify the virtual team's composition, create a virtual team composite picture, determine a name for your virtual team, and brand your team's work with its name.

75

Create new ways of managing conflict.

Rather than relying on age-old approaches such as yelling at one another or giving someone the "silent treatment," find new ways to manage team conflict and deal with differences.

One option is to encourage team members to first determine what they *agree* on rather than what they disagree on. After identifying areas of agreement, move on to points of disagreement and explore options for effectively managing the disagreement.

76

Assess the work that has to be accomplished.

If you are the manager of the virtual team, the team's output is uniquely within your sphere of responsibility. Know the projects that your team is tasked with and the status of those projects.

77

Challenge each person on your team to be a self-starter and a strong communicator.

These two key skills differentiate individuals who will succeed within a virtual environment from those who will be less-than-productive. Recognize and reward those individuals who can size up a situation and work through it effectively, keeping you and other members of the team informed as to what they did and why they did it.

78

"Mega-communicate."

Virtual relationships often lack the nonverbal communication opportunities that are present in face-to-face relationships. For that reason, verbal communication has to be expanded by a factor of 3 or 4.

Encourage 360° communication: to you, from you, to team members, from team members, to and from others not on the team but whose involvement is key to the team's long-term success, and to and from your team's customers.

79

Blend cultures and back-grounds on your virtual team.

A virtual environment is ideal for blending diverse backgrounds and abilities. By having a rich mix of skills, talents, orientations, and cultures, your team should be able to see problems and opportunities from multiple perspectives and thereby obtain high-quality results.

Such a blending will also require strong skills in listening, problem solving, and collaboration, which will also be beneficial to your team's work.

Make the transition from managing time to managing projects.

By focusing on projects, you ensure that your team is managing its most important asset: its output and its reputation.

81

Provide regular assessment of progress toward goals and objectives.

Feedback is the fuel of virtual teams. As in the case of communication in general, it is best when this feedback is complete in its format and design.

Encourage virtual teammates to provide feedback on and assessments of projects, milestones in the completion of projects, and other key activities that relate to your team's success.

Technology and Virtual Teams

Because of the nature of a virtual team's work, technology is an essential element in the team's tool kit.

Technology, however, advances far too rapidly to be captured in a book. For that reason, this section will examine fundamental principles of technology. A number of online resources are better suited for offering specific technology recommendations useful to virtual teams. Consult these sites for product-specific information.

82

Give team
members access
to tools that
support highly
interdependent
work, such as
advanced group-
ware or video-
conferencing.

The range and options of such tools increase on a daily basis. Assign someone on your team to become the resident expert on the tools and technologies that could be of use to your team. If your organization has a technology group that supports your team's work, so much the better. Determine if someone in that group can develop expertise (if he or she doesn't already possess it) in groupware and videoconferencing that might be useful to your virtual team.

83

Create a "virtual water cooler" within an electronic communication system to informally share information and perspectives

about what is going on with regard to individuals on the team or the team's work.

Informal ways of communicating will help your team feel like a team. Whenever an opportunity exists to share information relevant to the team or its members, use this "virtual water cooler."

84

Create tracks and footprints in physical space.

Establishing an audit trail for work that has been done will be useful to your team in replicating completed work.

Where possible on projects that have been completed, conduct "post mortems" using documents or presentation software. This will help others who might want to learn from your team's or sub-team's results.

85

Learn how to use a variety of electronic communication media strategically.

When is the best time to use videoconferencing? When is the best time to use e-mail or the telephone? Examining these topics within your team is likely to generate ideas useful to the whole team.

This discussion should also provide an opportunity to talk about the appropriate use of these tools and media. Make sure your team members know how to use these tools well and provide feedback that could be helpful in sharpening team members' skills in the use of these tools.

86

Use the phone more often.

In the midst of the highly electronic age in which we live, it is possible to forget one of the most basic tools we have for electronic communication: the telephone. The telephone still holds great potential for virtual teams—especially when cell phones, pagers, and PDAs are considered. The availability of these devices makes it possible for your team to stay in touch nearly 24/7.

That being the case, your team will also benefit by creating some rules for the use of phones and other communication devices during off-hours.

87

Switch media for greater impact.

There was a time when everyone complained about junk mail, but now we just tune it out. A similar numbing effect is happening with scores of phone calls, e-mails, and other electronic communication.

Change media periodically to create a fresh way of sharing information.

88

Create and use virtual conferences often to introduce or share expertise.

Live conferences offer fresh insights and new perspectives on issues and interests. So do virtual conferences. Virtual conferences, though, can be conducted at any time; all you need is an expert and an audience. These virtual conferences also provide an opportunity to highlight the individual expertise that is represented on the team. Leveraging that expertise for the benefit of the entire team makes wise use of resources, energizes and motivates the team to acquire new skills, and enhances the organization.

89

Use the grouping feature of e-mail software to increase the effectiveness of the virtual team.

Communicating to all members of the virtual team becomes easy through the use of the group feature of most e-mail systems.

Identify someone on the team to assume responsibility for the maintenance and distribution of an up-to-date list. This person will be responsible for promptly adding new team members to the communication loop and removing team members who leave the team from the distribution list immediately.

Use virtual meetings to handle specific near-focus issues quickly.

As in all meetings, focus on the goal of the meeting and the key questions or issues that need to be addressed quickly. Then engage in open dialogue on the questions or issues until the team is able to arrive at a solution.

91

Adapt decision-making software to facilitate problem solving and decision making.

There are a number of effective decision-making and problem-solving software tools available today. Choose one that fits in with the team's tasks and level of skills and expertise.

92

The more you interact by voice, text, and audio, the more you will be able to overcome the barriers of time, distance, and culture.

Virtual communication is becoming more and more popular as people become more comfortable with the technology.

Encourage regular use of this technology until your team has developed a high level of comfort and expertise.

93

Consider
the cost.

New technology does not come free, but it pays off in terms of long-term productivity and team effectiveness.

Before purchasing additional technology, conduct a cost-benefit analysis and select what will provide the greatest benefit at the most manageable cost.

Systems and Virtual Teams

Systems can be thought of as the factors that operate behind the scenes to assist the virtual team in doing its job well. Many of these systems are maintained by human resources, but not all. Technology is a part of these systems as well, but since technology was included in its own section, it will not be addressed again here.

For purposes of this section, "systems" refers to selection, hiring, training, developing, appraising, rewarding, promoting, and terminating. In short, "systems" includes everything that enables your team and your team members to function at the highest level of performance.

94

Establish the appropriate quantitative and qualitative data for accurate assessment of virtual team members.

Proper measurement systems will assist everyone connected with virtual teams to assess their effectiveness. Whether you are a team member, a team leader, or a customer of a virtual team, how the team performs is the key measure of its effectiveness.

What are those factors that should determine how well the virtual team is doing from the customer's perspective? From management's perspective? From the team's perspective? All these factors should be considered as you identify measurements and gather data in support of an effective team assessment.

95

Develop a thorough understanding of e-mail, tele-conferencing, and video-conferencing.

Each team member should be thoroughly familiar with the use of these tools and should be capable of using these tools at the appropriate times.

Conduct regular training and re-training in the use of these tools. Consider the development of job aids that might assist team members in knowing both *when* to use one of these tools and *how* to use these tools most effectively.

96

Compensate creatively.

What measures are currently used to determine how individuals are compensated? How effective are these measures within the virtual environment? Give careful attention to these tools and obtain the input and perspective from team members as to what constitutes high quality work within the virtual environment.

In addition, seek the support of a compensation professional who can offer alternatives to traditional approaches to compensation.

97

Reconsider performance management.

Since the team can't be under the watchful eye of the manager or supervisor, how should performance be measured and managed?

Part of the answer to this question lies in other areas that have already been considered (i.e., goal setting, communication, project performance, etc.), and part of the answer might be to overhaul current performance management systems so that these systems are more appropriately suited to a virtual environment.

After this process has been completed, ensure

that all members of your team understand the modified approach to performance management and are able to address the essential elements that will determine how their performance is evaluated.

98

Examine and revise your reward structure.

Most individuals perform at a level consistent with the rewards offered. What is the current reward structure in use by those on your virtual team? Is it working? Does it create the type of results that are needed by the team? If not, revise it.

If the structure does appear to be producing the desired results, review these factors periodically to ensure that they are still producing the outcomes needed by the team.

99

Consider the factor of system selection.

Appropriate technology is technology that effectively addresses the task needing to be accomplished, the organization's capability of using the technology well, the short- and long-term costs, and the users' skills.

Avoid the temptation of choosing technology with the most "bells and whistles," especially if it does not adequately address the factors listed above.

100

Thoroughly consider how you store your documentation.

The number of projects undertaken by your virtual team might provide a challenge with regard to storage. Where should the projects themselves or the electronic files be stored?

Make a decision and ensure that everyone on the team understands how data will be retained and, when necessary, retrieved.

101

Actively evaluate and reevaluate all the systems that affect the virtual team.

The rapidity with which technology changes poses a challenge for virtual teams and virtual team results. Those things that might have once been state-of-the-practice soon become "old news" and irrelevant. For that reason, it might be useful for you to identify and task a team of individuals to periodically review all the systems affecting your virtual team so that the most up-to-date and useful tools, technologies, systems, and practices are in place.

This continual review process will ensure that your virtual teams continue to achieve the outstanding results of which they are capable.

What's Next with Your Virtual Team?

It's 9:00 on the first day of the fourth quarter. Do you know where your team is?

If you are like many managers, your team may function, largely, on automatic pilot. They do the things that they may have done for years. In some cases, they hope for new results (as if producing mundane actions produces miracles), while in other cases they may be struggling to determine which end is "up" and how they can best go about addressing the increasing demands of a world that seems to be topsy-turvy.

If you add to this mix the fact that your team is spread out throughout the world, creating effective teamwork becomes far more than playing a round of "best ball" golf or white water rafting in West Virginia. True teamwork will require a deeper level of clarification, communication, commitment, and consequences management than is typically present in teams sharing a location. Teamwork must become more than a notion; teamwork must require the *team* to *work*.

The ideas presented here have been useful to distributed teams operating virtually and to teams that may not be distributed across various time zones. But the ideas will not work if they simply lay in the book! There is no magic in the book. The power of this book lies (literally) in your hands, as you determine how you will put into practice those ideas that can meet the needs of your organization.

With that in mind, check out the last two recommendations, included at no additional charge! I hope that they will be useful in getting you off of the sidelines of your team and into the game of creating team*work*. That's where the power is.

102

Identify five actions from this book that are critical to your virtual team's success and create an action plan for their implementation.

103

Share this book and the actions contained herein liberally with those who share the responsibility for the success of your virtual teams.